The Cardboard Shack Beneath the Bridge

Written & Illustrated by Tim Huff

CASTLE QUAY BOOKS

The Cardboard Shack Beneath the Bridge

Copyright © 2007 Tim J. Huff
All rights reserved
Printed in Canada
International Standard Book Number: 978-1-897186-09-1

Published by:
Castle Quay Books
1-1295 Wharf Street, Pickering, Ont., L1W 1A2
Tel: (416) 573-3249
E-mail: info@castlequaybooks.com
www.castlequaybooks.com

Written and illustrated by Tim J. Huff
Copy editing by Marina Hofman
Proofreading by Janet Dimond
Layout and design by Diane Roblin-Lee, byDesign Media
Cover Design by Tim J. Huff and John Cowie, eyetoeye design
Printed at Essence Publishing, Belleville, Ontario

Library and Archives Canada Cataloguing in Publication

Huff, Tim, 1964-
   The cardboard shack beneath the bridge / written & illustrated by Tim Huff.

ISBN 978-1-897186-09-1

1. Homelessness--Juvenile literature. 2. Homeless persons--Juvenile literature. I. Title.

HV4493.H83 2006   j305.5'692   C2006-905433-9

CASTLE QUAY BOOKS

Foreword

I met Tim Huff for the first time during my term as the lieutenant governor of Ontario. He was my guide on a tour of the underbelly of Toronto's night life, during which he took me to visit a relatively small area beneath a city expressway. I learned that countless homeless people may live there at any given time, many in makeshift shelters similar to the shack he describes in this remarkable little book. Tim knew nearly all of the residents of the expressway's underworld by name, and his willingness to look out for their well-being was the stuff of street legend.

We live in an age of unprecedented prosperity, yet people walk the streets of our cities, hungry and with no place to go. Many are young people, escaping from frightening family circumstances, and are homeless through no fault of their own. They suffer loneliness and despair, caught in the tragic spiral of homelessness and hopelessness. While there are many selfless individuals like Tim, who have dedicated their lives to helping people survive and get off the streets, there is a desperate need for concerted action from all of us if we are to tackle this tragedy.

I believe this book helps lay the groundwork for such action, by enabling parents and teachers to talk to children about destitution and poverty, and to help them understand the lives of those who are reduced to living in cardboard shacks and panhandling from strangers. *The Cardboard Shack Beneath the Bridge* gently raises questions in language a child can understand, and leaves it to the adult reader to steer an important discussion about poverty in our society. Tim's tender drawings and simple prose are the ideal guideposts; it is up to us to follow where they lead.

Hilary M. Weston

The Honourable Hilary M. Weston, C.M., O.Ont.,
Lieutenant Governor of Ontario 1997-2002

A Message From The Author...to Parents, Teachers and Caregivers

Several years ago my young daughter and I were walking from a downtown sports stadium to our parked car. We passed a makeshift shelter. Then shortly after we passed by an abandoned sleeping bag. A bit further, a man sleeping beneath a shrub. My daughter had many questions about what she saw.

Though I have been active in full-time outreach among homeless and street-involved people my entire adult life, even *I* had a difficult time choosing my words and answering her questions.

A short time later, on a similar jaunt with my very young son, I was put through my paces again. And once again I had to think carefully about the answers I gave. What words would be gentle enough, and still truthful? Which responses could both educate honestly and encourage compassion? This book is born out of the thoughtful curiosity of my own precious children. This book is realized by my years of experience among homeless youth and adults, along with the shared input of many of my friends: agency and mission leaders and frontline workers, professional educators, parents and grandparents.

As you read through the rhyming stanzas and take in the colourful illustrations, my hope is that you feel these are safe words and authentic images you can feel confident in sharing with the children in your care. As you revisit the content using the "Sharing Pages" discussion guide, my aim is that you feel equipped with information and child-friendly questions that will allow your child, your children, to explore their own tender hearts. And perhaps yours too.

One final thought...inevitably children will ask, "Why are people homeless?" or "How do people become homeless?" The most common stereotype is that young people are homeless because they are rebellious, and adults are homeless because they are lazy. This is not true. As you do your best to respond to the difficult questions children may have about the "whys" and "hows," be assured that the delicate truth is that the major contributors to homelessness in North America are: abuse, addiction, alienation, family breakdown, mental illness and neglect. Complex issues to discuss at any age. Ones respectfully left to your discretion.

As you might imagine, this book is dedicated to my children, Sarah Jane and Jake, who teach me incredible life lessons every single day.

This book has been created in honour of my friends on the street. I pray always that you are blessed in new and miraculous ways, just as I have been blessed with the astounding opportunity to share in your lives.

Tim Huff

5

ignored disappointed

lonely missed nice

srespected tender fired

forgotten human sad

gentle homeless hungry

precious surprising afraid

nique talented alone

6 priceless special cold

Author's Acknowlegements

It is impossible to touch on the individual names of all the people who consistently pour into my life in so many meaningful ways. However, among them, these caring and talented people enthusiastically shared their input and creativity regarding this book: Julia Beazley, Steve Bell, Laura Jane Brew, Carol Brown, Karen Clausen, Cathy Dienesch, Michael Frost, Sharon Gernon, Adrienne Grant, Mel Hems, Arlene and Liv Huff, Diane Huff, Sue Kocaurek, Sarah Lester, Jennine Loewen, Karen McCullough, Sister Sue Mosteller, Dion Oxford, Greg Paul, Heather Ploeg, Shelley Rumball, Colleen Taylor, Rick Tobias, John and Trish Wilkinson, and France Young.

My warmest thanks to the Honourable Hilary M. Weston for her great kindness and generous spirit.

My sincere thanks to Larry Willard at Castle Quay Books for his steadfast commitment and enthusiasm.

For special gestures of support, and/or for helping process creative ways to make this project happen, my thanks to: David Adcock, Miller Alloway, Alan Beattie, Gord Brew, Dave Collison, Martin Dockrill, Sarah Dumbrille, Mieke Geldart, Bob Gernon, Andrea Gordon, the guys in the band (John, Pete and Steve), Mark Kocaurek, Andy Levy, Sean Luxton, Kathy and Reynold Mainse, Bill and Gail Masson, John and Lori McAuley, John Mohan, Carl Nash, Pat Nixon, Dorothy Patterson, Linda Revie, Paul Robertson, Steve and Mary Ellen Rowley, Derek Rumball, Leslie Scrivener, Don and Fay Simmonds, Benita Hayes, Susan Henderson and Ginny Lyon at Weston Memorial Jr. Public School, and Marla Konrad, Clayton Rowe and Dave Toycen at World Vision.

Many thanks to my inspirational friends at Ark Outreach, Crossroads, The Dam, The Daily Bread Food Bank, EFC, Frontlines, The Gateway, Hannah Taylor and The Ladybug Foundation, Harvest House, Hockey For the Homeless, Inner-City Youth Alive, Mission Services of London, Muskoka Woods, The Mustard Seed, One Way Inn, Ontario Camp of the Deaf, Ottawa Inner-City Ministries, Salvation Army, Sanctuary, Scott Mission, Second Harvest, Siloam Mission, Sketch, Weston Park Baptist Church, World Vision, YFC chapters across Canada, USA and worldwide, Yonge Street Mission and YSM's Evergreen.

It is an honour to serve among people who faithfully give so much of themselves. Thank you to the incredibly devoted Light Patrol team, the entire Youth Unlimited staff (Toronto YFC), board, and our inspirational leader, John Wilkinson, as well as the many supporters who have stood with me in countless ways, for many years.

Thank you to my dear parents, my brothers and their families, and the Johnson family – for their continuous love and support.

And of course, thank you to Diane, Sarah Jane and Jake – for lovingly sharing "home" with me.

The cardboard shack beneath the bridge

Is hard to understand.

8

Does someone live inside of it?

A woman? Child?
A man?

Someone you may never know,

May never

sêê

or meet,

Used things they found to make a place

To think and sleep and eat.

It may look **dark** and very small,

Unlike the home you know,

But made for shade, and feeling safe

It blocks the rain and snow.

The person there is "homeless."

Perhaps there's more than one.

Perhaps there's more than one.

Perhaps there's more than one.

Perhaps there's more than one.

Perhaps there's more than one.

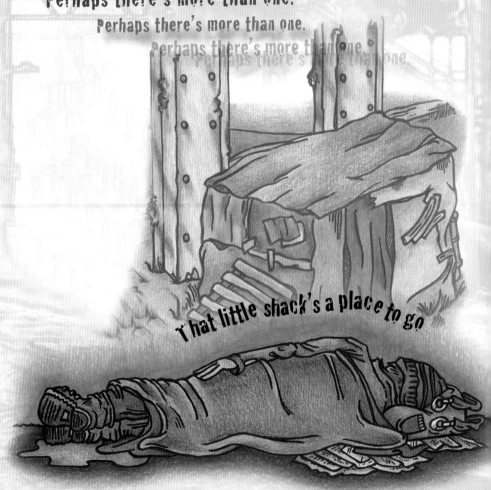

That little shack's a place to go

When their long day is done.

Have you ever asked someone,
"What does homeless mean?"
Well, here's a chance for you to learn
About what you have seen.

It means to be without a "home"
And live a different way;
Get by, and try to do your best
To make it through each day.

Without TV or fridge or house,
Is really just the start;
No doubt, without a family,
That is the hardest part.

15

Now as you gr**OW**, and learn and know
How grown-up things occur,

This book will teach you some new things

That you can know for sure!

No matter what you see or hear,
One thing is always true:

Each one without
a house and home
Was once a child like you.

Beneath the bridge or on the street

They all had hopes for more.

The hopes and dreams within their hearts

Were wishes just like yours.

While some need shelter, food or clothes,
Some simply want a smile.
And if you're with a grown-up,
You may just talk awhile.

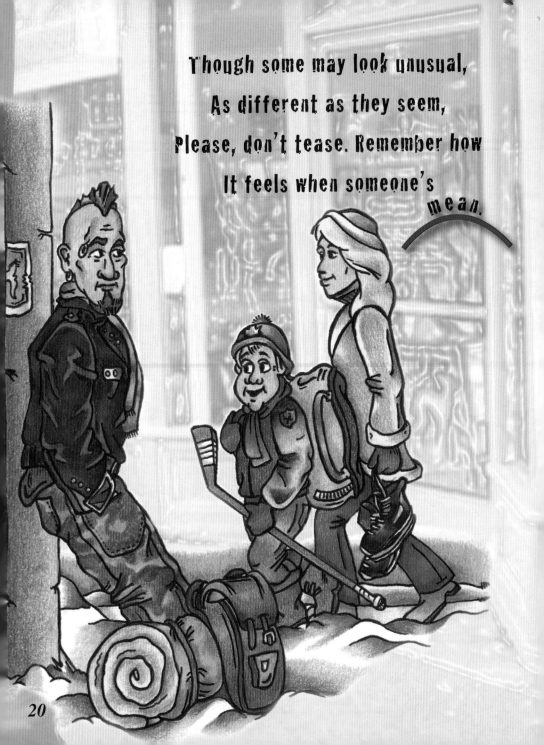

Though some may look unusual,
As different as they seem,
Please, don't tease. Remember how
It feels when someone's mean.

20

There's so much more still yet to say,
But this is a good start;

To pray, and say
you'll do your best
To keep them

in your
heart.

With love and care, God made us all,

And no two quite the same, but

All are precious in God's sight,   Each story, face and name.

For Grandma, Grandpa, Mom or Dad,
Perhaps it starts with you.
With gentle hearts, together ask,
What else can we all do?

Discuss it with your teacher
And share it with your friends.
Be kind. Remind your family
That caring never ends.

The cardboard shack beneath the bridge,
As strange as it all seems,

We can't forget that someone lives

Beneath those big steel beams.

passionate love

generous daughter u

kind mommy   school

e teacher helpful e

randma friend son

daddy thoughtful and

ister church brothe

caring gentle

Sharing Pages

A Discussion Guide for Parents, Teachers and Caregivers

Page-by-Page Discussion and Information Helps

Page 9. Sometimes, under bridges or near the main streets of cities or towns, you will see things that look like cardboard or wooden shacks, or even old tents. Perhaps you have seen an empty sleeping bag along with someone's belongings, tucked away in a place that looks a bit scary. Who did you think might live or sleep there? How did you feel when you saw it?

Page 10. Some people who are homeless choose to go to places known as "shelters" – where there are often several other homeless people. Most shelters provide a bed to sleep in and healthy meals, and have kind and caring people to help. Still, some people who are homeless feel nervous in shelters and are afraid or feel uncomfortable being around a lot of other people. Or they just want to be alone. Those are usually the people who search for odds and ends to build places like the cardboard shack beneath the bridge, or who choose to sleep outside. Why do you think someone might feel nervous or uncomfortable being around other people, or want to be alone? Have you ever felt that way?

Page 11. What do you think it would feel like to sleep outside on the sidewalk or hard pavement in the cold rain or snow, or in a cardboard shack instead of in your bedroom?

Page 12. For some people who are homeless, making a little shack or setting up a little tent is simply a way to feel a bit safer and dryer than sleeping out in the open. What do you think you would do – or where do you think you might go?

Page 13. In this picture you will see a man with his hat in his hand. He is hoping that someone might give him some money. That is often called "panhandling" or "panning." Some people think that is okay, and may give a few coins. Many people are uncomfortable with it, and do not like people asking for money. Whether you and the grown-ups you are with decide to give someone money or not – it is always good to smile and let the person know that you see them. That shows "respect." Have you heard that word before? What do you think respect means?

Page 14. Here you will see that the two men in the picture are sitting with their dog. Often people who are homeless have pets. If you were homeless, would you want to have a pet? Why? How might a pet be helpful? Is there any reason why having a pet might not be a good idea for a person who is homeless?

Page 15. Often people think the hardest part about being homeless is being cold or hungry, and not having your own warm bed to crawl into at night. Those are very difficult things for sure. But being lonely and sad can feel just as bad, or even worse. Why do you think that is true? How do you think you might feel? Do you ever feel lonely or sad?

Page 16. As you get older, you will understand better why some people are homeless, and how they end up living under bridges, in parks, on the streets, or in cardboard shacks like the one in this book. It is best if the grown-ups who care for you and look after you are the ones that explain some of these things. They will know when it is best. It is okay to not understand everything right away. You may already have some ideas about why some people do not have homes. Maybe you could talk with the grown-up you are looking at this book with about why you think some people do not have homes.

Page 17. It can be difficult to imagine what teenagers and adults were like as children. But remember, all of the young people and grown-ups you see who are homeless were your age at one time. Thinking about that helps us to be more "thoughtful" towards them. What does it mean to be thoughtful?

Page 18. What do you want to be when you grow up? What do your friends or brothers and sisters want to be, or want to do? The people you see who are homeless had dreams and wishes when they were children too, just like you. And you know what? They still do.

Page 19. You should never stop and talk to any stranger without a grown-up that you know and trust at your side, or without their permission. But if you get a chance to safely talk with someone who is homeless, often it is such a pleasure for that person to get to speak with you – even if just briefly. Many are very lonely. Sometimes even just saying "hi" and smiling can make anyone feel good. Do you ever have times when it feels good to have someone cheer you up, just by being friendly?

Page 20. Sometimes a person who is homeless may look a bit scary to you, or some people may even seem to act a bit differently than what you are used to. Not always – just sometimes. Of course some people look very friendly and kind too. And usually they are. Either way, never embarrass or make fun of people, no matter how they look or behave. How do you feel when someone teases or makes fun of you?

Page 21. Have you ever heard someone use the big word "compassionate"? What do you think compassionate means? When people are compassionate it means that they want to care for others and often want to help in some way. Being compassionate is very good, even when you do not understand all of someone's problems. Sometimes it is hard to know the best way to help others. But remembering people in our thoughts and prayers is a big part of being compassionate, and can sometimes help us know better how to help or be involved in other people's lives.

Page 22. You are special! There are many wonderful things about you that are like no one else in the world. Remember that every person is very special – no matter where they live or what they look like. Who do you know that thinks you are special? Why do you think that they feel you are special and important?

Page 23. There are many ways people can help others who are homeless. There are groups (sometimes called "organizations") that are friends and caregivers among those who are homeless. There are also many churches, places of worship and community programs that help and care lots too. There are many good people who work and volunteer in these places and with these groups. Some provide food, warm clothes and shelter. Some provide friendship. Some provide special help in finding ways to not have to be homeless. Some do their best to help with all of these things.

Do you know a place or group in your city or town that helps people who are homeless? If you do not know where or how you can help, maybe you and a grown-up can find out together. Can you think of some thoughtful ways that you can help, or show that you care?

Page 24. Parents, grandparents, teachers, and all kinds of adults who care for you teach you many important things every day. But sometimes you can teach things to grown-ups, and to your friends too – with special reminders about caring and being kind to other people. Is there something new that you have learned from this book that you want to be sure to remember, and maybe tell others about?

Page 25. When you look at the last picture in the book, of the person in the doorway of the cardboard shack beneath the bridge, how does it make you feel? Whether you feel sad, worried, bothered, scared or upset, it is always important to remember that those who are homeless are real people – just like me and you.

972